ALIVE ALIVE O

Greta Stoddart was born in 1966 in Oxfordshire. She grew up in Belgium and Oxford before going on to study drama at Manchester University, then at the École Jacques Lecoq in Paris. She co-founded the theatre company Brouhaha in London, touring the UK and Europe. She has lived in Devon since 2007.

Her first collection *At Home in the Dark* (Anvil Press, 2001) was shortlisted for the Forward Prize for Best First Collection 2001 and won the Geoffrey Faber Memorial Prize. Her second, *Salvation Jane* (Anvil Press, 2008) was shortlisted for the 2008 Costa Poetry Award. Her third collection is *Alive Alive O* (Bloodaxe Books, 2015).

GRETA STODDART

ALIVE ALIVE O

BLOODAXE BOOKS

www.bloodaxebooks.com
For further information about Bloodaxe titles
please visit our website and join our mailing list
or write to the above address for a catalogue.

Supported using public funding by
ARTS COUNCIL
ENGLAND

Cover design: Neil Astley & Pamela Robertson-Pearce.

Digital reprint of the 2015 Bloodaxe Books edition

And her ghost wheels her barrow
Through streets broad and narrow
Crying cockles and mussels, alive, alive-O!

Molly Malone, traditional Irish song

ACKNOWLEDGEMENTS

Acknowledgements are due to the editors of the following publications where some of these poems first appeared: *Long Poem Magazine*, *Magma*, *The North*, *Ploughshares* (US), *Poetry London*, *Poetry Review* and *The Spectator*.

'The Curtain' was published in *The Best British Poetry 2012* (Salt Publishing, 2012).

Very many thanks go to the Helyars, Josh Ekroy, Don Paterson, and especially to Helen Evans, for their critical readings of these poems.

'Deep Sea Diver' was shortlisted for the Forward Prize Michael Donaghy Best Single Poem 2012.

CONTENTS

The Curtain

Perhaps you know that story where people step
out of this world and into another
through a split in the air – they feel for it

as you would your way across a stage curtain
after your one act, plucking at the pleats,
trying for the folded-in opening through which

you shiver and shoulder yourself
without so much as a glance up
to the gods, so keen are you to get back

to where you were before your entrance:
those dim familiar wings, you invisible,
bumping into things you half-remember

blinded as you'd been out there
in the onslaught of lights, yes, blinded
but wholly attended to in your blindness.

Imagine our dying being like that,
a kind of humble, eager, sorrowless return
to a place we'd long, and not till now, known.

No tears then. Just one of us to hold
aside the curtain – *here we are, there you go* –
before letting it slump majestically back

to that oddly satisfying inch above the boards
in which we glimpse a shadowy shuffling dark.
And when the lights come on and we turn to each other

who's to say they won't already be
in their dressing room, peeling off the layers,
wiping away that face we have loved,

unbecoming themselves to step out
into the pull and stream of the night crowds.

Stars

Our dead do not congregate
but appear to us, distinctly, as they were:
her sharp brilliant self, his gentleness,
that darling girl's sly smile,
which could be why when I have them meet
in heaven or here at night in my room,
they make absolutely clear
in the way they don't open their mouths
their disdain at my – what is it – it's my hope
that in the enormous mutual oblivion
in which they find themselves,
they'll all get on.
They always appear too proud or sad,
too detached in their deadness
like they're trying to work out how space is measured,
like they want their distances back.
Oh, let them walk the six long miles to Shute Barton,
let's watch as they swim their lengths of gasping spraying butterfly!
But they can't. They can't even move.
They're just there, burning up the past.

Lifeguard

Of course I know he meant nothing to me
alive, why would he, a part-time lifeguard
at the local pool I'd only ever glimpse
slumped in a plastic chair or standing deep
in a cupboard leaning his chin on a mop.
The only thing that passed between us
was a look – almost cold from us both –
when I asked him for armbands, the hard kind.
He handed them to me as if I wasn't there.
The day he died I drove past Skindeep
and saw him outside on the pavement, smoking,
squinting in the late afternoon sun,
his shaved head, his stumpy legs.
Yes, I remember thinking, that fits, that crew –
pierced, tattooed, the hair (too much or none), the bikes.
And glancing in the rear view mirror I saw
the line of his head almost golden in the dust.
A few hours later I walked into the pool foyer
and there, to one side – a sheaf of lilies
in a mop-bucket and a small table
where a few sweaty carnations were scattered
around three photos in a plastic sleeve:
one of him looking very small on his bike;
another he must've taken himself, it had that
mild looming look of a fish swimming up
to its own reflection; and one of him
hunched over a naked back, needle in hand,
with such a look of care and concentration
I almost felt his breath on the back of my neck.
People were walking past and buying tickets.
Someone was explaining about off-peak times.
It'd been one of those suddenly hot days

at the end of March and there was something high
and reckless in the air. I'd seen a woman
at the lights with huge long breasts in a low black top
and men with their tongues practically hanging out
and I remember thinking here we go again
and the kids in the back were squabbling and my thighs
sticking together and I wanted only to dive into the pool
though I'd never learnt how and wondered
was it too late and who would I get to teach me?
The road kept on before us, hot and black.
I thought of how big and smooth his face was
as if his features hadn't quite finished forming
though already punched with studs and rings and chains
and his eyes seemed swollen and full of something
like he'd cried a lot as a baby, or not enough.
He never looked at us. I remember thinking
how could this man save us? How would he know
if one of us just stopped and slipped down
on to the tiled floor? He'd look out across
our blue bright shrieking square
but never at us. Not in the way he is now
like the dead do from their crowded lonely stations
and I'm looking at him in a way I never did
when we lived in the same time, same town
with its narrow streets and muck and diesel air.
Now, when he appears there on the pavement,
smoking and squinting in the light, I see
evermoving water, a slab pinned and still,
a body submerged, a body pierced.
But then, when the lights changed and I pulled away
(let me say this now and without pride) I had you
drugged and disaffected, unfucked and aimless
and I marvelled with some bitterness how someone like you
could ever be sleek and forgetful and strong
in the clear blue streams, could ever have the grace

or urge – however vague – to save a life.
How was I to know I'd just seen a man
in his last light, taking time out for a smoke,
a final look at old Fowlers' smashed windows,
its drape of red ivy and dry weeping nests
an hour or so before he swung a leg
over the new bike, dropped the visor down,
wound his way out in the low evening sun
to the A28, the Little Chef bend, the lorry.

Lamb

The crows were black
coming to and to it
and the dog barking
was black and the trees
standing in a row
behind it were black-
trunked black-branched
and a black plastic
bag hung
torn inside
the black spaces
and the puddles were black
with mud and ice
and the leaves were black
and the lamb
the crows and the dog
wanted so badly
the lamb with its small
white splintered
hull of a chest
sticking out
so emptily
to the wind
you could almost
hear in the bony
tines a tune
the lamb was the dead
this early spring
the dead centre
of everything

Daughter

So they were called to come in and watch
her moony thorax slapped up on the lightbox
show how a small shadowy gathering
had appeared in the dim garden of her lungs.

Home, and sitting at the long wooden table
where she'd lie to receive their daily trembling
dose of heparin, where now lay a Bible,
he said *I want to be able to forgive them.*

Gethsemane. Moonlight. And the mob
– armed to the hilt, alert to the kiss –
who knew only what they had to do
and never mind who suffered
for how long or in how many ways,
came and took the beloved child away.

Deep Sea Diver

There's a field inside my head

It's dark and flat and a moon hangs
above it in whose silvery light
nothing appears to live

It's very mysterious and simple,
on a different planet

to this one here
that moves and is manifold:

each one of the tens of millions of blades of grass
shivers in its singularity

one sheep's crusty underwool is home
to a greenbottle settling down to lay
her two hundred and fifty possibilities

while another stares out
of the glazed globe of an eye

not unlike a man who's lost his mind
but found there cause instead
to be vaguely, dully, afraid of everything

And beneath the sheep
and field and flattened buttercups,
miles and miles beneath

all is shift and shale,
burn and boil

Old underearth,
unseeable, unexplorable

who scrambles through your soft weak rock,
who swims through your molten ocean,
what holds court at the centre
of your solid iron ball the size of the moon?

Once I plumbed down
level by level

into the sea,
into the realm

of the falling debris,
dead and dying-fish-eating creatures

into the freezing black waters
of blind long-tentacled things

down among the deepwater canyons I went
and still nowhere near was I

to the outer core
of the earth's interior,
its massive indoors

when I saw hanging there
a sole, or flounder

a self never before seen

but one who remained unchanged
in the bright beam of my look

And I rose to the surface
like one who had only that to do

where slowly over the years
all that I held dear came loose

and I took to the fields
that covered the earth
like so many soft dressings

and I lay down and looked up at the sky

where I saw a fish hanging
in the black, where I saw a moon

Voicemail

And as I left the message
I realised that you
were probably already
dead – a fact my voice
seemed to know before I
did as it dropped
right down
and started slow to speak
– a strange tone, very
slow and uninflected
as if an arrow could fly
with a heaviness
but straight, knowing
exactly as it moved
through a long blackness –
it knew, for example,
not to say
Happy New Year
how in the not saying
the truth rang clear –
that there'd be no year
or month or even a week
that you'd had your day
and your soul had outrun
you in the night, was in
the running now forever –
something my voice
seemed to know before I
did when it stopped
hung up
and didn't say goodbye

And here you are

         among us again
telling us – with that accuracy
and hilariously – what it was like,
wide-eyed, exhilarated to have been there
and now back here in a room again;
you here in a room again
with us all standing around grinning,
filling to the brim
to have you among us again
raising our glasses
to your unbelievable absence

ICU

The nurse who's just turned off the machine
walks out with such a sorry little smile
I want to stop her and say,
'Hey, I was watching that!'

We stand around in our big coats.
He looks very bare in a white vest
and perfectly capable – having a kip
in the sun before seeing to the sheep.

But he won't be going anywhere,
not tonight, not in this cold.
What should we do now? Touch him.
It feels – how quickly it went – cold.

Then we're back in the beige room
with the box of tissues and water jug,
the empty hills and blue lakes,
the room that became – so quickly – ours,

where we were told, very gently:
The head, you see, has received such a shock...
Imagine the brain as a sponge, it can only take...
Who's supposed to finish these sentences?

Not us, surely – we barely know
what day of the week it is.
All we know is what we see
in the empty hills and blue lakes.

Here comes the bereavement lady.
She stands there with a large brown envelope.
The way she looks at us I can tell she's sorry
for how sorry we look, not for our sorrow.

I walk over to the window
and look down at the ring road
and beyond it a green field
with rows of headstones.

Standing behind this triple-glaze
in this small hot disinfected space,
I wonder how could anything get out,
how could even the *idea* of a soul –

I think of the empty hills and blue lakes.
I think of our car parked somewhere.
Someone must've parked it.
Was there a ticket? How will we find it?

Turning back to the room
they call the Relatives' Room,
I see a man and his mother.
I see through their coats and shirts and things

to their white bewildered bones
and swift obedient blood.
I see into their aliveness
there on the sofa.

Where is your husband now, where your father?
In a dark room that had to be left.
We had to leave it. We had to leave
that dead face to its dead self.

All those turning

Blow you wild in the wilderness
   you all who the ever you are
you once of the world – whirl round
   it now – whip more and more
into the blear and blaze
   of your ever-ending circle

Blow you spirit-wind you soul-gale
   you who so searingly outnumber us
howl and haul in all those turning
   now to dust – to this hot wind
this planet's bright belt
   of charged streaming dead

Blow you blinding storm
   you wind of nothing
to the naked eye – turn up the high
   white hum of the invisible
ring made up of all manner
   of things lost to us

Blow you gone
   you still and never-to-be-born
you dead for a century dead for a day
   all you outliving us out there
in the catastrophic air
   of this black and never dawn

See how you blow you bone
   spark you ash-turned air
into this room where I stand
   with these small shaking waves
in this glass of water
   I hold in my shaking hand

Interior

There was thunder outside. I was inside making beds. It was four o'clock in the afternoon, it was dark. I pulled the thin brass chain on the bedside lamp and the room filled with yellow light. There was thunder outside. I was inside making beds. I heard a train go past. I saw this window from the train – a square of yellow light – and thought What's happening inside that room? Or is the room empty and only by its glow suggesting something that isn't there? There was thunder outside and I was inside making beds. And the thunder was nothing but air above a patch of earth coming to big warm blows with itself and I was nothing but a mass of atoms bending and folding and smoothing. Between us nothing but a wall. And just as I was leaning into a warm waft of powder and sweat a huge electric burst set big dry waves cracking across the sky and the air elbowed its way expanding quickly pushing apart great invisible swathes of particles. What's out that's not in? Thunder outside and me in pulling a sheet tight, tucking and folding in the yellow light and the chain swaying very slightly and the sound of thunder – or was it a thought – bounced off the ground having nowhere to go and I was nearly done here, lifting the last sheet, flapping it out for the clap and the crack. What's in that's not out? Me inside making beds. Thunder outside moving on.

House and Train

I

When I see our house from the train
as it glides away on the spot where it sits
in its patch of scrub and thistle
and gone-over kale, its flappy shed
and rain-thin chickens;

when I see its wide-eyed four-windowed face
and tall redbrick chimney
and around it all a stone wall
where cows come to rub their necks,
I'm the only one who knows

there's a young dog buried
under that sheet
of corrugated iron;

a dead man's watch
lies buckled and ticking
in a little green jug on a dresser

and in a box under a bed
a page in a child's hand:
There once was a girl...

I know about these things even,
or especially, at this distance
and the house manages
to keep it all in without
a single alteration to its footings.

It's other stuff – the earth's heaves,
swallows' nests and southwesterlies,
cracking clay and an oak's roots,
the thick-necked intractable cows –
that little by little break it down.

II

this is the one you close you
say to keep out the cold but
really it's that bird you want
to stop the one which won't
itself come in but is surely
out to get you with all that
singing and singing

this is the one that leaks and
leaks it weeps in the face of
all that light and cloud in
the face of all those gulls
sweeping the fields and all
the flooded valley it weeps
in all the grey brightness

this one needs cleaning with a
rag that was once part of a
shirt a man would wear while
axing logs and all around
snow would fly and each flake
be only vaguely deferring its
sudden soft extinction

this is one with no glass just
a few bars thick with rust and
dirt – a dark hole keeping to
itself its chains and hooks
and old blood keeping to
itself its dream of ancient
cattle

III

But look at that one there, lit up and passing, passing
quickly *on its way on its way*, look at that girl facing
herself in the night, looking so hard into the glass she
might be looking into herself when really all she wants
to see is out; how safe she looks there on the quiet side
of the glass, she's handed herself over so completely,
the seat, the speed, even that paper are not hers and
nothing will stay still long enough to hurt her.

IV

I watch the houses slide away
and see how they all contain

the same different things;
each has that same sealed look.

But some have spilled out catastrophically.
It's been impossible to keep it all in.

Whose is that busy broken garden,
whose that desolate neatness?

And who are those two people
facing each other inside that room?

They don't feel a thing.
They are simply in out of the cold;

it's warm and they have chairs
to sit on and think about things

happening somewhere else
to people they really don't know at all.

They are quite involved and cheerful.
They each have the same black cup.

This was us in Maths

feet up on the desk, talking back
to watery-eyed, greasy-haired Miss.
How the class laughed!
What kings we were!
Then your dad died.
And I couldn't go near you
or look you in the eye.
I couldn't write a note
or cycle round
and post it through your door.
And this was your chair:
upright and empty and me
staring out the window
over the slate roofs
and jostling tree-tops,
over the muddy school field
and two lonely goal-posts,
over the wide road
and humming cars,
over all this and more,
on and on, all the way
to your house that stood
at the end of a long cul-de-sac
where I imagined you
lying on your back
lifting your hands
(your right wrist
with its ganglion
I used to love
to push down
and watch slowly rise),
lifting your lovely long fingers,

seeing them turn
in the light and dust,
having yourself all to yourself,
so much more now
than ever you were with me,
in all your sadness, Susanna,
in all your glory.

Fallacy

To a baby what is it but a shawl of light,
a draught gentling through the rungs of a cot

but the child shuffling to school is the first
to smell the dying in the black wet leaves

which could be why she finds herself breathing
all day and deeply from her new pencil-case

and when she strikes further out
across this land of rinsed light

as long as the wipers flog their thudding
measured beat, she'll be consoled

and soon she'll hold it all inside herself:
the raindrop, the wind's blunt ecstasy,

the snow that comes to grant every thing
its silent wish. I mean her, her silent wish.

Letter from Sido

So, my very dear mother, speak on the verge of death,
speak in the name of your inflexible standards, in the
name of the unique virtue that you called 'true elegance
of behaviour'.

COLETTE

I'm writing this by the light of a barn
in flames, Madame Moreau's. One wonders,
with the old man gone and her gout getting worse.
I see the poor rats running all over the garden.
How beautiful it all is!
I saw old Loeuvrier go by last week
in his coffin. I do like watching funerals,
one can always learn from them.
But don't ever let me see you in mourning for me,
you know how I loathe black – what's wrong with pink?
I've been making a big bed-jacket from an old pink quilt.
I want to be buried in it. Thank you for your invitation.
No, Josephine is *not* sleeping in the house.
I sleep here alone, so please, no more fuss.
No more stories of wicked tramps kicking down the door.
Give me a dog if you like.
Ever since your father died I cannot bear
another human being in the house at night.
Dear child, you write that you're not well,
is it the city, the air too thick and sour?
Do you remember that time I went to the Curé
in a fury about something only to dance home
with that beautiful Pelargonium cutting he gave me?
This time he gave me a cactus – it's here on the sill.
Beyond it I can see the blaze dying down.
I keep waking up. The other morning at three
I watched a very handsome garden spider slowly

descend and drink from my blue bowl then draw
herself, heavy with chocolate, back up to the ceiling.
Et voilà! a new companion.
I've been going through the books on your father's shelves.
It's such a bore – all the love in them.
In real life, my poor Minet-Chéri, folk have better things to do.
I hear from your brothers – so you write about your life?
You see? I warned you about going to confession,
I always said it led a child to play around too much
with words, make things up, navel-gaze.
Better to hold your tongue – punish yourself yourself.
This cactus is very rare. It's pink.
And the Curé says it's about to come out.
As I write, a stray is winding her way round my ankles.
She looks quite blue in the glow. I'll cook her an egg.
I did the same for poor Yvette's girl the other day.
I don't do it because I'm good, heaven knows.
I do what'll set my mind at rest – you know me.
The other day I found a caterpillar hibernating,
a bird had pecked out her stomach.
I have her healing now in a little matchbox of sand
on my bedside table – what a beauty she'll be
and all the more so for having suffered!
There's just black sky now where the barn was.
You know the worst thing about being old?
– the sight of my hand on the sheet.
I still play chess with my little wool-seller.
Your father would have been delighted,
the dead are a peaceful company, my child.
The Curé tells me this cactus only flowers once
every four years. And I am dying.
You will forgive me, won't you, Minet-Chéri,
you will understand that I can't come to you.
You who took three days and three nights to leave my body.
Children like you are the most beloved because

they've lain so high, so close to the mother's heart.
I can hear my pen scratching in the dark.
I have grown very thin.
When I'm at the water pump in the morning
I feel my dress touch the backs of my legs,
the sun is just warm and I feel ten years old.
How can I leave now?
How could I leave that thing to flower alone?
Someone needs to see it into the world.
I want it to be me peering into its closed pink heart.
I want to watch it push its slow suddenness
out and quiver there in the warm air.

Robin

The other day it was my friend
who hopped from wall to bench,
who stopped and cocked his head,
his eye bright and black with asking
Why, why are you still crying?

Today it is my dear young drunk
of an uncle in that thornbush
outside the kitchen window,
peering in, wondering where
I've hidden the Scotch.

What the Gardener knows

Here he comes with his hope and dibber,
his plastic labels and permanent pen

for the slow spacing out of seeds
under the glass roof, the sky roof

though he knows, poor man,
green shoots up no matter what

into the whole and open air
of each unbroken morning

like this one here with its mist
moving in with a stillness

around the trees, the trees
who know – because they are rooted

even in all this vagueness –
exactly what they are

which is more and ever (evermore)
and what the gardener knows is

there's a certain amount of time
for the garden to be made

new again and for a man
with his little tray of wobbly seedlings

to step into it and be,
by this fool and happy business, saved.

Poet

There was the soft white shock of hair
as he came carefully to the lectern,
his body – post-stroke – blown open
and now only delicately connected

There was the old thistle I pulled up
this morning, all rot and root,
its hollow stalk ridged and sodden-brown,
its blackened crown

The man who stood before us in that hall,
the clear reed of his voice, was one who knew
that *all must be harvested and yielded*
no matter what – each word a seed,

a small outplosion,
a pouring away into the wind

Wild Pear

And
so it
hung
there
like
a
dull
jewel
which we
picked with
out a thought
and tried to bite
but our teeth just
slid down its skin
The sun was warm
so we sat it on a wall
where it lived through
days of wind and rain and
then – we forgot about it – ice
and snow until in spring our boy
came to us holding up the shallow
bowl of his palms and there it was: no
silvery fur or bird peck no fast-ruining
bruise – just the cold grey drop of itself
(or perhaps just the slightest tooth mark)
What was this thing that wouldn't green or
yield or soften or rot   more stone than fruit
form than flesh – we held it gently because
of the wondering but really there was no
need – this is what it was to be
past caring – this single
hard unadulterate
tear

Mud and sun and stone and rain

I could've walked right up to her
and stroked her gunky brow,
wiped the green drooling from her mouth
but all I did was stand and look
at the suffering, the self-annulling of it:
This is not happening, I am not here,
even you looking at me will not bring me to this.

I wanted to know what it was like
inside the dying – was it a slow slowing
down to a slippery quick frantic dark then
a stop – and what was it like to leave
with no allegiance to others:
to the other sheep or sad-faced farmhand,
the low brown swoop of fieldfares at dusk?

Or was she feeling herself sliding towards
the edge of the world and then to
its final ledge
of mud and sun and stone and rain
off which she'd tip and gently roll,
her black hooves dangling,
soft-barrelling her way into space?

Next morning I saw her laid-down shape.
I could see she was done with
her slow dispassionate cleave from the world.
Now she was safe all right, for a long
night had passed and bunches of bloody fleece
had bloomed under a fat harvest moon
where her neck had been half chewed off.

Spiders

Like something blurted out
    and absolutely
not intending to take itself back it
    appears there
one day on the bath floor
    where it stays and stays

many-eyed but seeing
    through its eight long legs
and brown bristled abdominal body.
    I feel it
all tense and brooding
    in its defensiveness.

I'm not one of those who
    can just come and scoop
up a palmful of frail panicky life
    and fling it
without a thought down to
    the wet leaves below

but – hello – next morning
    there's another one
exactly the same but smaller, paler.
    Family.
And I've this vision
    of them all palping up

the damp hair-cushioned pipe,
    dragging their spinners,
threading their thinly segmented legs up
    and out of
the depths of the black hole.
    I push the plug in.

Next day I look there's five;
    not so much kin now
as pioneers, arrived some long hard way
    to try out
this new empty land
    where there's little food but

(thanks be) a continual
    drp drp of water
and lots of warm connected crawlspaces
    underground;
yes, quiet, resilient
    as missionaries.

There's something female
    about the sixth one,
huger, softer – come, as ever, at night;
    with her here
you know this is home.
    But how're they getting in?

I stare down into the
    wide bathy bleakness
and see just above the dirt horizon
    the row of
broken Jacuzzi holes:
    eight dry safe nest-bowls.

All day something rises
    up through me till I'm
full and irresistibly decided;
    yes, I will
bundle them all up
    in a towel and rush

to the window – go, out,
    fling, disperse, balloon,
go wind your ancient know-how in the air!
    Then I'm back
turning the taps on full,
    watching the water

level rise tremblingly
    like a hand barely
able to hold down what's coming up, this
    mindlessly
limpid uprising,
    this simple filling up.

I imagine a wall
    of water held there –
shivering, bright, ecstatic! before it
    crashes down,
collapsing like a –

    Oh look, here they come now
with their little ones,
    their drenched clogged bodies
balled up, circling, in a slow washed-up tide

Effigies

How many of us have meant
only to look in –

hook the window out a notch
slot a foot back in
under the eiderdown –

and ended up staying there
in the just-enough dark

to listen we say for breath
when really we stay

for the thrill and dread we get
from looking at them asleep

a sleep where they are growing
without a sound and beautiful

where they are growing old

before our eyes
beyond their years

by stillness perfected

before a mumble and stretch
that small impatient sigh
collapsing them back to life

– what love they burn when at their most dead!

Space

Because you've done
most of your deep sleeping
and will soon come into the clear
grey page of morning

and because nothing has been
as yet thought of or spoken
in this small-roomed hour
it can take up all the space

and your children –
who are for now asleep,
who have for now placed
their hot soles against the wall –

could, for all you know,
feet-first and dead to the world,
be wanting back
into that black space

where our half of the earth
hangs spinning;
this is where it does its singing
– can you hear it?

It doesn't want you to be afraid
though in this hour,
this close to it,
how could you not.

Give it a face if you like,
no, don't, because it has no face
and you know it
is more foot-fall in the dark

and you're more like
the astronaut on his watch,
condemned to a view
of the earth as a ball

wrapped up in itself
(and quite small),
in its wind and weather,
its millions of dreaming selves.

Turning Earth

We know how hard a year is

                we who grieve

how much the turning earth hurts

                how absence

likes to present itself in the light

                of each new season

you dead in spring is not the same

                as you dead in winter

but you alive was you alive

                oh all the year round

And then there is the night

                which is its own season

the slow dark that comes always

                suddenly upon us

a black room in which we wake

                and feel the fact that you

who were so complicatedly here

                are now so simply gone

Show

There's been a flurry of things
falling this past hour
as I've sat here in my chair:

a mild tornado of leaves,
crow's theatric plunge
and now out of the grey

large, largely-spaced snow
coming down with a no-sound
that gives to each fall...

These flakes are what words would be
if we never spoke them,
coldly constantly dying out

but turning to rain they return things
to their good sound spirits
which means it's time to get up

out of that dumb show
where all was space and hypotheses,
see to what needs doing

in this world of rain
but know what fell before to earn
this thoughtful, continual applause.

The Line

I

This is them
without their selves

upside down, headless,
them hung

by their ankles and cuffs and toes
(Where have they gone?)

sorry as flags
in the doldrums

unable to signal a thing
save the wind's withholding.

I peg it all out
in this little order I have:

huge shirts and work trousers,
a row of small and smaller vests.

Why I, so pushed for time,
seem now to have it all –

but there's something heraldic
about these colours and shapes and patterns;

this tending to such forms
a kind of summons

as when I look on them asleep
and there they are, all spirit gone.

II

into the weave   of nylon and wool
there comes the damp   air from the woods

into the cotton   jersey and lycra
comes the branch-rich   root-rich

air from the woods

and up through the valley   a wider air gathers
dust from the corn   cut   and the quarry
dust from fur   and a fistful of feathers

and into each fabric   into each fibre

comes air translated   sweating oil
acrid-thick   from muck

and out from the Undercliff's   stony old air
come iron and clay   peregrine breath

within it the lime   within it the laurel
within it the foxmould   and scree

and rising cool rising cold   comes river air
in see-through layers   of silt and scale

and into each fabric   into each fibre
comes air

chopped by Chinooks   come chunkingly low
whirred by the whirring   whirring of birds

and into each fabric   into each fibre
comes air   land has breathed
and sun has stared   through

and through   holes and slits
collars and sleeves   through legs and arms

flapping like wings
air that blows   and dries and sings

III

I come out at dusk and there
they are, cold and slightly stiff
now evenings come on so quick

I pick them off, fold and pile them up
in the old log basket
I hoik for the walk back

For the moment on the step
where I turn to face what I can't see
in the gathering dark

And in the day's slow dissolving
I see a thrush
bashing its meal on a stone

Can almost hear
the clod and carcass-eaters
blinding about in the earth

Before I back into the house
where lights are blazing
and boys are charging about

Where it's all happening

Frame

We sit around a bed inside a room.
The corpse is laid out like a kind of light.
It's the only thing we can bear to look at.

We can't move. We can't imagine stepping
out of here and carrying on –
When all of a sudden last night appears:

the red room, the fire's wild shadows,
my boys stripped to their waists, wrestling,
the shine of sweat on their faces.

It's like a painting. Its one frame
glances off many-angled now, its light
comes from inside and very far away.

Boy with Candle

Look at you, sitting there
hunched over your candle,
grinning like the devil
at his latest defiance.

You've come to that age:
slamming doors, sleeping late
and now this – passing your finger
slowly through a flame.

What say you to fire
being, in our hands, a protest
against the night, the cold,
the fear we tend to in ourselves?

You slice the flame over and over.
I want you to stop. Take it.
I want to watch you, son,
leap up and hop, howling, to the sink.

Skull and Hourglass

Hold them there inside that golden room,
their faces flushed, their bellies full of food
and that girl's (surely, look at her smile) with love,
settling its milky pool in some pelvic nook;

hold that man, hale and loud, laughing
down the cleavage of some woman not his wife
whose small black eyes look out at us as if
we might know the secret of her life.

Hold them there before
the old sorrow creeps in
over the bleared plates and sticky glass,
the exhausted cloth, before the night has lost

all it promised at dusk when the swans
shone their loneliness out on the black lake.

Fire on the beach

The sun was burning
low into the sea
turning the beach into the long burnt memory of itself

when we set about
building a fire with whatever
came to hand: chip paper, crate splinters, half a rusty lighter

and when it was as good as done
we lit and lowered a match
to a brittle coil of kelp.

And as it took we watched
the flames pulse and shy,
breathed in the briny saltsmoke and weedcrackle

and the longer we looked and lost ourselves the deeper
we seemed to be staring
into the core of the sun

even as we turned
from her and she from us, leaving us to huddle in
with our shield of hands

around this nest
of orphan flames,
one of billions spitting out across the earth.

And when the dark
came cloaking in from the sea and covered our backs
and cut the rocks and boulders black

we kicked the fire down dead in the sand
and felt ourselves pulled
by the hard light of the moon in our bones,

by our own long shadows, back up to the car
leaving behind us the hiss and grate
of the sea on the stones.

NOTES

Letter from Sido (36)

This is a collage of a poem. Some lines have been taken or changed from letters and memoirs from two of Colette's autobiographical books *Break of Day* (translated by Enid McLeod, Capuchin Classics) and *My Mother's House* (translated by Una Vincenzo Troubridge and Enid McLeod, Penguin). Some lines are made up. I have put them all together in this imaginary letter from mother to daughter.